ONLY IN MISSISSIPPI
A Guide for the Adventurous Traveler

ONLY IN MISSISSIPPI

A Guide for the Adventurous Traveler

LORRAINE REDD

QUAIL RIDGE PRESS
Brandon, Mississippi

Dedicated to
Mama & Doony
Evelyn and the late S. F. Redd

Library of Congress Cataloging-in-Publication Data

Redd, Lorraine.
    Only in Mississippi: a guide for the adventurous traveler/
Lorraine Redd.
        p. cm.
    Includes indexes.
    ISBN 0-937552-54-2: $5.95
    1. Mississippi--Guidebooks.   I. Title.
F339.3.R43   1993
917.5204'63--dc20   93-32607
                                                      CIP

QUAIL RIDGE PRESS
P.O. Box 123 • Brandon, MS 39043
1-800-343-1583

Photos by author, unless otherwise noted.
Cover and graphic design by Karen Wing.

Contents

INTRODUCTION

Traveling the backroads, searching for the unique and unusual, has always been a favorite pastime. When sharing the experiences of weekend roadtrips to Earl's Art Gallery or Margaret's Grocery with friends, many wanted to know how to get there. Thus, the idea for *Only in Mississippi* was born.

Only in Mississippi is not the definitive guide of the state, but if you're looking for an uncommon travel experience, you're holding the right book. This guide will take you way off the beaten path, and introduce you to some of the most colorful and authentic people and places in Mississippi. Many of these sites you won't find listed with the local chambers of commerce and, before this guide, might have only heard about through word of mouth. From the nostalgic to the bizarre and everything in between, this insider's guide will escort you to home-grown museums, artists and craftsmen, Elvis and blues sites, the few remaining country stores and drug store soda fountains, and to restaurants that have good food and character to match.

Just a few traveling tips before you hit the road. Get off the interstate as soon as possible because from that vantage point Mississippi looks like a sea of pine trees, dotted with service stations. If you really want to see the state, you'll need to get on the old highways, which often run parallel to the interstates. Or just turn off down a country road. It's hard to get lost in Mississippi, and even if you do, it won't be for long. Besides, there's no telling what you might find. Traveling to many destinations in this guide takes time and planning. Most of the museums and personal collections are open to the public by appointment only, so don't gamble that folks will be home. You are likely to be disappointed. Many people do not charge admission to see their artwork or collections, or to sing you a blues tune, but they will accept donations. Please be as generous with your donations as they are with their time. Also, travelers should not be surprised if businesses do not keep the exact hours listed in this guide. Mississippi is a casual and laid-back place, and many people temporarily set aside business affairs when hunting season or the Neshoba County Fair rolls around.

From the Gulf Coast, up through the piney woods region and the Delta, to the red-clay hills of the north, Mississippi is a huge territory for one person to cover thoroughly. Undoubtedly, there are more creative folk artists, skilled craftsmen, quaint museums, and colorful restaurants that would merit inclusion in future editions of this guide. Your suggestions are welcome and can be mailed to me in care of: Quail Ridge Press, P.O. Box 123, Brandon, MS 39043.

For additional information about traveling in Mississippi, call the Tourism Division of the Mississippi Department of Economic and Community Development at 1-800-647-2290. For information about state parks, call 1-800-467-2757.

ACKNOWLEDGMENTS

Special thanks to Jack Davis for encouragement and advice; thanks also to Sharon, Jamie, Lauren, and Amanda Bush; Anna Furr and family; Karen Wing; Rae Nell and Bill Presson, Jennie Francis, Stacy Doolittle; Phyllis Alexander; Delarie Maddox; Martin Mangold; Dave Miller; Guy Land; Stan Magee; Walt Grayson; Bill Ferris; Denton Gibbes and Judy Rhodes Davis with the Mississippi Department of Economic and Community Development; the staffs of the Mississippi Department of Archives and Eudora Welty Library; and my loyal traveling companion, Hanna.

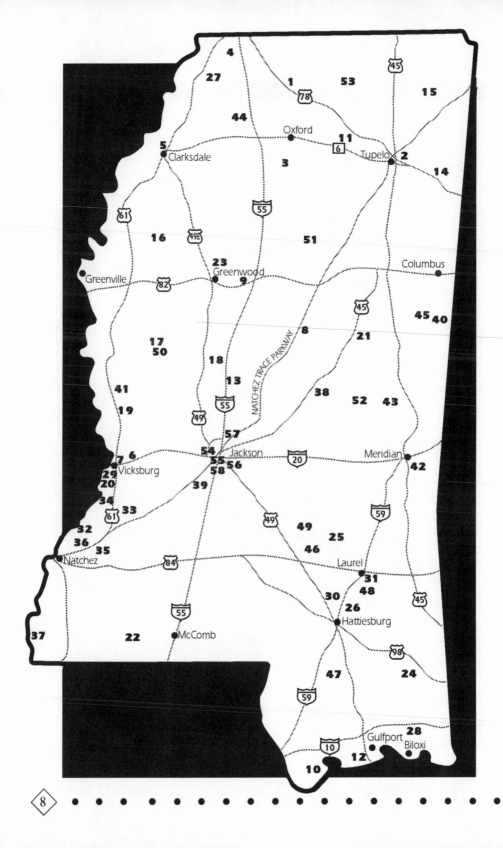

ELVIS

1 Graceland Too, Holly Springs
2 Birthplace of Elvis, Tupelo
3 Mike McGregor's Shop,
   Lafayette County
4 Honeymoon Cottage, Desoto County

5 THE BLUES

FOLK ARTISTS

6 Earl's Art Gallery, Bovina
7 Margaret's Grocery, Vicksburg
8 Mrs. Hull's House, Kosciusko
9 Jewel Thomas, Carrolton
10 Alice Moseley, Bay St. Louis

ARTISTS & CRAFTSMEN

11 M.B. Mayfield, Ecru
12 Gulf Coast Art Community
13 Greg Harkins, Vaughn
14 Peppertown Pottery, Peppertown
15 The Quilt Gallery, Burton

MUSEUMS

16 American Costume Museum,
   Ruleville
17 Ethel Mohamed Wright Museum,
   Belzoni
18 Booker-Thomas Museum, Lexington
19 Buddie Newman's Museum,
   Valley Park
20 Dr. Lindley's Veterinary Museum,
   Vicksburg
21 American Fire Museum, Louisville
22 Jerry Clower's Museum, Liberty
23 Prayer Museum, Greenwood
24 Palestinean Gardens, Lucedale
25 Watkins Museum, Taylorsville
26 Checker Hall of Fame, Petal

PERSONAL COLLECTIONS

27 Country Charm Antiques & Museum,
   Eudora
28 Beer Container Collection,
   D'Iberville
29 Corner Drug Store, Vicksburg
30 Arrowhead Collection, Seminary
31 Model Train Collection, Laurel

GHOST TOWNS...sort of

32 Rodney
33 Rocky Springs
34 Grand Gulf

COUNTRY STORES

35 The Old Country Store, Lorman
36 Wagner's, Church Hill
37 Pond Store, Wilkinson County
38 Bryan's Grocery, Freeny Community
39 H.D. Gibbes & Son General Store,
   Learned
40 Bigbee Valley General Store,
   Noxubee County
41 Onward Store, Onward
42 Causeyville General Store,
   Lauderdale County

MILLS

43 Sciple's Grist Mill, Kemper County
44 Cobb's Sorghum Mill, Sardis

FARMS

45 Sunshine Farms, Noxubee County
46 German Baptist Community,
   Covington County
47 Batson Log Cabin & Fish Farm,
   Wiggins
48 Trapper's Gator Farm, Jones County

EVENTS

49 Watermelon Festival, Mize
50 World Catfish Festival, Belzoni
51 National Sweet Potato Festival,
   Vardaman
52 Neshoba County Fair,
   Neshoba County
53 First Monday Trade Day, Ripley
54 Chimneyville Craft Festival, Jackson
55 Dixie National Livestock Show,
   Rodeo, & Western Festival, Jackson
56 Mississippi State Fair, Jackson
57 Canton Flea Market, Canton
58 Jackson State Homecoming Parade,
   Jackson

Paul and Elvis Aaron Presley MacLeod

THE KING'S MEMORY THRIVES IN MISSISSIPPI

Graceland Too

"The World's Number One Elvis Fan" resides in Holly Springs, halfway between Graceland in Memphis and the Elvis birthplace in Tupelo. Paul MacLeod and his son, Elvis Aaron Presley MacLeod, are at work diligently preserving the memory of the King of rock and roll. They've transformed their antebellum home, Graceland Too, into a personal shrine to honor America's beloved cultural icon, and unlike many others who have immortalized him, the MacLeods have done so through their vast archive of Elvis information.

The MacLeod collection represents one man's life's endeavor, and it continues today in partnership with his son. The collection ranges from original recordings, to tickets from Elvis' last concert, to petals from the first flowers placed at Elvis' grave. Most unique at Graceland Too is its archive. It includes an impressive 19,500 newspaper clippings and 2,000 newspapers making reference to the King. Twenty-four hours a day, 365 days a year, father and son take turns manning six televisions and two VCRs, duly video-taping and cataloguing anything Elvis. To date, six TVs have been casualties of their work. Disc jockeys from around the country shouldn't be surprised to receive a call from the King's "Number One Fan" if they dare utter the slightest inaccuracy about Elvis. At any hour of the day, the Holly Springs duo are likely monitoring the airwaves with their shortwave radio.

You don't have to be an Elvis fan to find a tour of their home an unforgettable step into the phenomenon that Elvis created. Graceland Too is located at 200 East Gholson Avenue in Holly Springs and is open Monday - Sunday, 12 pm to 8 pm. Admission - $3.00. (601) 252-7954.

TUPELO-THE BIRTHPLACE OF ELVIS

Annually, thousands of Elvis Presley fans from around the world make a pilgrimage to Tupelo to visit the hallowed birthplace of the legendary Mississippian. On January 8, 1935, Elvis was born in a two-room shotgun house that his father built in 1934 with $180 he borrowed. The house was repossessed a few years later, and the Presley family lived in several other Tupelo homes before moving to Memphis in 1948. The Elvis birthplace is located at 306 Elvis Presley Drive, along with the Elvis museum and the memorial chapel, where fans go to meditate. Admission to the birthplace is $1.00; and admission to the museum is $4.00. Hours are 9 am to 5:30 pm, Monday - Saturday, and 1 pm to 5 pm on Sundays. From September to April, the grounds close at 5 pm.

Devoted Elvis fans may also want to visit other sites in Tupelo, such as the Assembly of God Church, where Elvis worshipped as a boy; Lawhon School and Milam Junior High, where young Elvis completed grades one through seven; and Tupelo Hardware, where he bought his first guitar. The Tupelo museum also displays a collection of Elvis memorabilia.

WAY OFF THE BEATEN PATH

MIKE MCGREGOR-LEATHER AND JEWELRY SHOP.
Elvis enthusiasts may also want to visit with Mike McGregor, former jeweler, leather craftsman, horse wrangler, and handyman for Elvis. At McGregor's shop on State Highway 7 South, between Oxford and Water Valley, you can purchase replicas of Elvis' trademark show belts and Elvis-inspired jewelry and leatherwork, as well as reminisce with Mike about his days in the King's court. (601) 234-6970.

THE HONEYMOON COTTAGE.
At one time, Elvis owned a 168-acre ranch in Desoto County, about ten miles from the gates of Graceland. He and Priscilla spent their honeymoon in the cottage on the property, located near the southwest corner of Goodman Road (or Highway 302) and Highway 301. The modest house is white with black shutters, and has several columns on the front. A family now resides in the home, so tours are not available.

Courtesy of The Mississippi Department of Archives & History

*The late
Son Thomas*

BIRTHPLACE OF THE BLUES

The Mississippi Delta, a 200-mile stretch of earth between the Mississippi and Yazoo rivers, is the land where the blues began. Around the 1890s, black musicians created a distinctive music that evolved from spirituals, field hollers, and work songs. From these humble beginnings, the blues went on to influence 20th-century American music, emerging in bass patterns, guitar riffs, and piano boogies in country, pop, jazz, and rock. The music of Elvis Presley, Mick Jagger, and Jimmie Rodgers resonates with sounds born in the Delta.

Highway 61, "the Delta's main street," courses through the heart of the region into the towns of Rolling Fork, Anguilla, Nitta Yuma, Panther Burn, Alligator, and Clarksdale—where you should begin or end your tour. Clarksdale and Coahoma County were home to famed bluesmen W.C. Handy, Charlie Patton, Robert Johnson, Son House, Muddy Waters, and Howlin' Wolf, who created a blues tradition that many locally known performers follow today.

CLARKSDALE

DELTA BLUES MUSEUM

Try to make your first stop the Delta Blues Museum in Clarksdale, where you can learn about the history and significance of the blues. The museum has a growing collection of videotapes, photographs, recordings, books, memorabilia, and other information about the blues. Located at 114 Delta Avenue and open Monday-Friday, 9 am - 5 pm; and Saturday, 10 am - 2 pm. Admission is free, but donations are encouraged. (601) 624-4461.

ZZ Top (left to right) Dusty Hill, Billy Gibbons and Frank Beard with the Muddy Waters Life Figure at the Delta Blues Museum

Courtesy of the Delta Blues Museum

STACKHOUSE/DELTA RECORD MART

Next, stop at the Stackhouse/Delta Record Mart. Jim O'Neal, owner and local blues expert, sells blues LPs, CDs, tapes, 45s, and 78s (reprints and originals) as well as blues books and memorabilia. If you are a serious fan, consider purchasing for $7.50 the Delta Blues Map Kit, which provides maps and descriptive notes to historical blues sites, burial sites, jook joints, and other points of interest. Located in Clarksdale at 232 Sunflower Avenue and open Mon. - Sat. 12 pm - 6 pm. (601) 627-2209.

THE RIVERSIDE HOTEL (Blues Hotel)

There are many hotels in Clarksdale, but for a real taste of the blues, consider staying at the Riverside Hotel. Originally Clarksdale's black hospital, the building became a blues landmark when Bessie

Smith, the Empress of the Blues, died there in 1937 following an auto accident on Highway 61. In 1944, Mrs. Z.L. Hill turned the building into a hotel and boarding house, and through the years, it has been the residence of many blues greats. Mrs. Hill, now 85, is a kind and gracious woman, who describes herself best when she says

with a warm smile, "I'm everybody's mamma." Her home is your home, as she puts it, and a visit with her is a delight. With its relatively modest accommodations, including common bathroom facilities, the Riverside Hotel is for the adventurous traveler. Rooms are $25 per night. Located at 615 Sunflower Ave. (601) 627-6294.

OTHER BLUES SITES IN AND AROUND CLARKSDALE

WADE WALTON'S BARBERSHOP–Owned by Clarksdale's famed blues-singing barber. He's a good source for finding out who's playing where, and he may even play a tune for you between customers. Located at 317 Issaquena Avenue. (601) 624-6067.

WROX RADIO–Central Building, 125 3rd Street, Room 222. (601) 627-7343. Early "Soul Man" Wright has been broadcasting here since 1947. Early's show features blues from 6 to 8 pm and gospel from 8 to 10 pm, Monday through Friday, and gospel on Sunday from 5 to 10:45 am. Visitors are welcome.

W.C. HANDY'S HOME SITE–A marker now stands where the home of W.C. Handy once stood. Located on Issaquena Avenue, near Third Street.

MUDDY WATERS' HOUSE–7 miles northwest of Clarksdale. Waters made most of his 1941-42 Library of Congress recordings in the house.

What remains of Muddy Waters' house

OTHER BLUES SITES IN THE DELTA

DOCKERY FARMS–Located on State Highway 8 between Cleveland and Ruleville, Dockery Farms is often noted as the birthplace of the blues. Early bluesmen Charley Patton and Henry Sloan lived on the plantation and passed the blues on to other residents, such as Willie Brown, Howlin Wolf, and Pops Staples. The barn is visible from the highway.

ROBINSONVILLE–A mixture of myth and reality surrounds the brief career of the legendary Robert Johnson, who grew up in and around Robinsonville. As the story goes, he left Robinsonville around the age of 20 as a fair harmonica player and a disaster on the guitar. A year later he returned as the best blues player in the land. It's said that he sold his soul to the devil for the ability to play the blues better than any other man. He died mysteriously at an early age and has been the subject of a major movie and books.

TUTWILER AND MOORHEAD–W.C. Handy first heard the blues around 1903 while sitting at the Tutwiler depot waiting for the train. As Handy later described the scene, a lean black man sitting nearby pressed a knife against the strings of his guitar and sang about "Goin' where the Southern cross the Dog." Handy's recollections represent the first-known documentation of the blues, as well as the slide guitar. The man was headed south to Moorhead, where the Southern Railroad crossed the Yazoo and Mississippi Valley Railroad, also known as the Yellow Dog. Historical markers now stand at this once well-traveled juncture, and where the Tutwiler depot stood.

JOOKIN'

If you want to hear live music, plan to be in the Delta on a weekend. The staff at Stackhouse Records and the Delta Blues Museum, as well as other blues enthusiasts you meet as you tour the Delta, can suggest jook joints that may have the best music. Booking arrangements for bands are often casual and impromptu, so it's best to call ahead, stop by the establishment in the afternoon, read posters on telephone poles, or just show up that night to find out if and when a band is playing.

BLUES FESTIVALS

The blues tradition comes to life on a grand scale at festivals throughout Mississippi each year. Call ahead to confirm dates.

Mississippi Delta Blues Festival (the state's largest blues event), held the third Saturday in September each year in Greenville. (601) 335-3523.

Sunflower River Blues Festival, the second weekend in August each year in Clarksdale. (601) 627-7337.

B.B. King Homecoming, generally held the first weekend in June in Indianola. (601) 887-4455.

Mississippi Gulf Coast Blues Festival, held in September each year in Biloxi. (601) 388-8010.

Farish Street Festival, held in September on the Friday and Saturday after Labor Day in Jackson. (800) 354-7695.

Northeast Mississippi Blues & Gospel Folk Festival, the second Saturday in September in Holly Springs. (601) 252-4661.

Courtesy of the Delta Blues Museum

B. B. King

TUNE TO THE BLUES

Saturday nights from 10 to midnight, tune into "Highway 61" on Public Radio in Mississippi (PRM), when "blues doctor" Bill Ferris plays the best of the blues. Bill is also the director of the Center for the Study of Southern Culture at Ole Miss, which publishes *Living Blues* magazine. You can pick up PRM just about anywhere in the state between 88.1 and 91.3 on the FM dial.

FOR MORE INFORMATION about blues sites in the Delta and other travel information, contact: The Clarksdale/Coahoma County Chamber of Commerce at (601) 627-7337; The Greenwood Convention and Visitors Bureau at 800-844-7141; The Washington County (Greenville) Convention and Visitors Bureau at (601) 335-5822; and the Indianola Chamber of Commerce at (601) 887-4454.

Earl Simmons

Air conditioning vents on the exterior of Earl's gallery

 • • • *Folk Artists* • • • • • • • • • •

EARL'S ART GALLERY
Bovina

In Bovina, a small community east of Vicksburg, you'll discover Earl's Art Gallery, which has been best described as the visual equivalent to the Delta Blues. The proprietor and artist is 38-year-old Earl Simmons. The combination art shop, museum, wanna-be restaurant, and home was created over a 14-year period from scrap lumber and other salvaged materials. For the $2.00 admission you can tour his museum, where you'll find artwork of Earl's own creation on exhibit, as well as family photos, newspaper clippings, and an old jukebox that he will play for you by lifting the top and pushing in an eight-track tape.

Despite limited financial means and no formal art training, Earl's creative spirit is unrelenting. It springs forth in his art which is raw, pure, and honest. He works with whatever material he can get, and gets it wherever he can. He turns scraps of wood and discarded household items, like lampshades and frying pans, into large model trucks, buses, and cars. But Earl paints as well. His strokes are broad and bright, and unmistakably his. Earl knows that recognition and success for an artist is usually a posthumous development. Earl, however, hopes to be an exception.

To get to Earl's, take the Bovina exit off I-20 near Vicksburg, follow the main road that curves around the service station, take a left at the stop sign and cross the railroad tracks, stay to the left when approaching the old red country store, and continue ahead. Earl's is on the left. (601) 636-5264. Earl's work is also sold at the Attic Gallery at 1406 Washington Street in downtown Vicksburg.

MARGARET'S GROCERY

Vicksburg

Eight years ago, Reverend H.D. Dennis told Margaret, "Marry me, and I'll turn your grocery store into a palace." She consented, and he fulfilled his promise. Located a couple of miles north of Vicksburg on Business 61, Margaret's Grocery stands immodestly in its unique architectural style.

The designer and builder, 78-year-old Reverend Dennis, or Preacher, as Margaret and their customers call him, is a World War II veteran who learned the art of masonry from the Germans. The principal lesson: "Don't build nothing like nobody else." He took that advice to heart and with brick, block, and mortar, turned Margaret's Grocery into a personal monument to God, country, and spouse. The colors red, white, blue, and a touch of yellow decorate castle-like pillars and archways at the store entrance and highlight the walls that surround the Dennis domain.

Reverend H.D. Dennis

Preacher has been a messenger of God's word for most of his life, and if the store now serves as his church, the gravel parking lot is his pulpit. Expect a lively sermon, and the opportunity to be "blessed" by touching the Ten Commandments, which he has inscribed in marble and houses in his rendition of the "Arc of the Covenant." Overlooking the parking lot, a tower of inexact design stands 50 feet high or more. Once completed the tower is where

Preacher plans to enshrine the Ten Commandments.

Divinely and personally inspired, Margaret's Grocery continues to evolve. "God keeps telling me," Preacher says in reference to the tower, "to keep going higher."

Margaret's Grocery is open seven days a week from 8 am to around sundown. No admission fee, but donations are accepted. (601) 638-1163.

Preacher atop his tower

MRS. HULL'S HOUSE
Kosciusko

Mrs. L.V. Hull always dreamed of "having something that nobody else had." When you see her home, you'll know her dream has definitely come true. Mrs. Hull, 50, undoubtedly has one of the most unusually decorated homes in the entire state, and maybe the nation. The front yard overflows with painted tires, shoes on stakes (that look like they've grown out of the ground like tomato plants), a computer, typewriter, and hundreds of other items she has collected and thoughtfully placed throughout the yard. The artistic arrangements continue inside, where her small house is bursting with thousands of trinkets and treasures. Mrs. Hull believes "an idle mind is the devil's workshop." If that's true, the devil gave up on Mrs. Hull years ago. This imaginative and jovial woman is a pleasure to visit, and she welcomes guests any time. Located at 123 Allen Street in Kosciusko. No admission, but donations are accepted. (601) 239-9227.

JEWEL THOMAS
Carrolton

As a child, Jewel Thomas, now 78, helped his father forge farm
tools in his blacksmith shop. From those childhood days he
developed an interest and love for old farm implements, and in the
1970s he started collecting them. Today, old plows adorn the fence
posts lining his property. Saw blades, tractor wheels, bottles,
hubcaps, gourds, an old limousine, and more all find a welcome
resting place as decorations for his home. Car tags from 36 states
cover one side of his garage, and he hopes to complete the
collection with tags from the remaining 14 states.

A retired pulpwood cutter and truck driver, Mr. Thomas says that
he is home "might near all the time," and he and his wife of 31
years, Lula Mae, enjoy having visitors.

To get there take U.S. Highway 82; if you are coming from
Winona take the first gravel road to the right past the Vaiden-
Highway 35 exit; coming from Greenwood, cross State Highway 17
and turn left at the first median crossing and go straight down the
gravel road.

Alice Moseley

ALICE MOSELEY
Bay St. Louis

When Alice Moseley was 61 she was spending hours of each day at the bedside of her ailing mother. To pass those painful hours away, she bought some paint, brushes, and paper and began painting whatever came to mind. Through her despair she uncovered a talent within that she never knew existed. So at 62 she retired from a 30-year career as an English teacher and began a new one as an artist. Now an energetic 83 years old, she has received much acclaim for her work. Each of her paintings tells a charming story of life in the south and they have amusing titles to match like, "Life Gets Tegous*, Don't It," "Three Sheets in the Wind," and "Git Up to Snuff; You've Time Enough." Her work has been described as "idyllic" folk art, because she shows what the artist prefers to remember, not necessarily what really was. Ms. Moseley feels that having no formal art training has been an asset. "I can do anything I please," she says. "Since I haven't been taught anything, I can't offend anyone."

Ms. Moseley lives in a quaint cottage at 214 Bookter Street in Bay St. Louis, which also houses her gallery. Prints and originals are available for sale. (601) 467-9223.

* Southern slang for tedious.

Cousin Kitty from the Crescent City

"Cotton Pickers" by M.B. Mayfield

M.B. Mayfield

M.B. MAYFIELD
Ecru

Born in 1923 in Ecru, M.B. Mayfield was the one who among eleven brothers and sisters was gifted with the eyes and hands of an artist. In his youth, Depression-ridden Mississippi formed images in Mayfield's mind that he has skillfully transferred to canvas ever since.

Although he lacked formal training, his natural abilities developed as he grew into a young man. The front porch of his house served as his gallery, and he occasionally sold his work to passersby. In July 1949, an art professor from Ole Miss spotted his work on the porch and stopped to speak with the artist. The professor recognized the innate talent of the 26-year-old Mayfield. Yet because he was black, he couldn't qualify for a scholarship, or even admittance to the all-white university. So the professor offered him a position as janitor and handyman in the art department. Once his chores were completed, Mayfield situated himself in the janitor's closet adjacent to the classroom, with an easel and art materials donated by faculty and students. With the door slightly ajar, he participated in the class. Thirteen years before Ole Miss was officially integrated, Mayfield was probably the first black to attend classes at the university.

Mayfield matured as an artist during the three years he worked and studied at Ole Miss. When the professor transferred to another university, Mayfield returned home to care for his ailing mother. After her death he moved to Wisconsin and then to Memphis, where he continued to paint and began to receive recognition for his work. In 1979, he returned home to Ecru.

Now 70, Mayfield continues to paint his childhood memories: Depression-era hardships, one-room schoolhouses, rural rolling stores, church services, funerals, and farm life.

He enjoys having guests, and if he has any artwork on hand it is usually for sale. Call before you go and he will give you directions to his home. (601) 489-2514.

GULF COAST ART COMMUNITY

From an automobile on Interstate 10 or U.S. Highway 90—the parallel concrete arteries that rush through the heart of Mississippi's Gulf Coast—the area can look like a blur of billboards, casinos, and fast-food restaurants. But turn off those roaring thoroughfares and

Shearwater Logo

you'll find what has inspired Mississippi fine artists for decades.

Make your first stop Ocean Springs. Going south on Washington Avenue from I-10 or Highway 90 will lead you to the oak-lined streets in the center of town. Turn left before the railroad tracks and visit the restored train depot, which houses two shops: one featuring the work of metalsmith and jeweler Gayle Clark; and the other, Realizations, Ltd., selling Walter Anderson prints and clothing emblazoned with the late artist's designs.

Courtesy of the Ocean Springs Chamber of Commerce

Virtually unknown in his lifetime, this reclusive and eccentric artist shunned conventional life to live close to nature. After his death in 1965, hundreds of pieces of his work were discovered, and many of his originals are now on display at the Walter Anderson Museum of Art at 510 Washington Avenue. Also on this street is Art Who?, a gallery nestled in a turn-of-the-century cottage showing a contemporary collection of art and fine crafts.

Jim Anderson

From Washington Avenue follow the signs to the rustic workshops and gallery of Shearwater Pottery. Situated on 24-acres of wooded land overlooking the Mississippi Sound, this unspoiled haven has nurtured the creativity of four generations of Andersons. The pottery was founded in 1928 by Peter Anderson, Walter's older brother, and continues today with the work of Peter's son, Jim, and other family members.

Next, head to Moran's Art Studio in Biloxi by going west on Highway 90 past the lighthouse and turning north on Porter Avenue. The studio is just off the highway on the right. The Morans are descendants of George Ohr, "The Mad Potter of Biloxi," whose turn-of-the-century abstract work was decades before its time. Considered the town lunatic by some, he could hardly give away his pottery. Today, one pot can sell at prestigous auction houses for more than Ohr earned in a lifetime. Several pieces of Ohr's pottery are on display at the studio, as well as the colorful oil paintings of Joe Moran depicting Gulf Coast scenes, and the work of his children Tommy and Mary Moran. Another intriguing exhibit is the ancient burial site of 13 skeletons, which can be viewed from the studio. Believed to date to 2200 B.C. to 1500 A.D., the skeletons were uncovered during repairs after the building sustained damage from Hurricane Camille in 1969.

George Ohr
and his pottery

George Ohr's work is also on display at the Gulf Coast branch of the Mississippi Museum of Art along with rotating selections from American and Mississippi fine artists. The museum is located at 136 George Ohr Street in "Old" Biloxi. Further west, in Pass Christian, lovers of art and fine crafts will enjoy a visit to Hillyer House at 207 East Scenic Drive, which features art, jewelry, pottery, and gifts from 175 artists from Mississippi and across the nation. Artists demonstrate their talent in the store each Saturday throughout the year. At 119 E. 2nd Street is the Raintree Gardens and Gallery, where beautiful, lush plants are pollinated with art and fine crafts.

Bay St. Louis, Mississippi's oldest incorporated town, is home to over 60 artists, many displaying their work in shops in the "Old Town" section of the community. Bay Crafts at 107 Beach Boulevard offers functional and unique crafts from Mississippi and American craftsmen; The Serenity Gallery at 126 1/2 Main Street features the work of over 50 Mississippi artists; folk artist Alice Moseley displays her work in the front room of her home at 214 Bookter Street (see page 27). A brochure listing 40 businesses in the district is available at many shops in the area.

HARKIN'S WOODWORKS

Vaughan

From an old country barn on Possum Bend Road, 40-year-old Greg Harkins skillfully crafts the sturdy oak rockers that have won him national acclaim. Four presidents, numerous celebrities, and hundreds of people from across the nation and a host of foreign countries have purchased his traditional chairs. He uses time-honored techniques passed down from Mississippi master chairmakers who taught him to build furniture to last. He takes no shortcuts and spends about 30 hours on each chair. From timber grown on his own property, he carefully cuts the wood so the grain is at the best angle for supporting weight, and hand-turns every wooden part of each chair. Cane seats and backs are hand-woven by local weavers. He offers several styles of rockers, and recently began crafting a new style of hickory furniture that preserves the natural lines and raw beauty of the wood.

To get there take I-55 to the Vaughan exit, and follow the signs, which will lead you to Greg's barn. If he's not at the barn, he may be at his home, which is just north of the barn. He can usually be found wherever his well-used, white truck is parked. (601) 673-8229.

PEPPERTOWN POTTERY

Peppertown

Titus and Euple Riley began making pottery around 1981 after Euple took two ceramics classes at the local community college. Titus wanted to make a butter churn and although they didn't know how, they tried and learned. The successful creation of that butter churn was the birth of Peppertown Pottery. From what Euple learned in her classes and what they taught themselves, they've built a thriving business. Using clay dug from a gravel pit in Itawamba County, they create a variety of decorative and functional pieces, including primitive face jugs, figurines, bird houses, and hushpuppy dispensers.

But the Riley's successful partnership began when they were just children. Titus and Euple were both born in Itawamba County, and

Courtesy of D. C. Young

made friends in grammar school. When she was 13 and he was 15 they became sweethearts. Two years later, in 1945, they ran off to get married. They found a preacher working in his orchard, and while still sitting in their car, he married them on the spot. Two years later, when she was 17, they had their first child and two more soon followed. Until the creation of Peppertown Pottery, Titus worked as a mechanic, farmer, and truck driver, and Euple was never far away.

After telling of their romantic beginning, Euple adds, "It hasn't been all peaches and cream, but we've made it through. If one of my grandchildren did the same thing today, I'd have a fit."

Peppertown Pottery is open Tuesday - Saturday from 8 am to 4 pm.   To get there take Interstate 78 to the Peppertown/Mantachie exit, which will put you on old Highway 78 north. Take the first left, which is State Highway 363, and Peppertown Pottery is 1/4 of a mile up the road on the right. (601) 862-9861.

Courtesy of D. C. Young

THE QUILT GALLERY
Burton Community

After a 31-year career as a teacher and principal, Claude Wilemon retired and now devotes himself full-time to his "hobby." That hobby developed about 20 years ago when Wilemon began buying and selling discarded scraps from the local textile mill to supplement his modest teacher's income. While working with a local seamstress to turn the scraps into a quilt, he found he had an eye for design. That first quilt sparked his passion for designing, collecting, and selling quilts. Although he's never sewn a stitch, he continues to work with local seamstresses to create both hand-and machine-sewn quilts of traditional and contemporary design. He has added rooms to his home to display his collection of several hundred quilts, all of which are for sale. He also sells quilting fabric at pennies above his cost, as well as pre-cut packets of scraps for numerous quilt designs. The Quilt Gallery is located in the Burton community east of Booneville on State Highway 30. The shop is open 7 am to 5 pm, Monday - Saturday. (601) 728-3302.

AMERICAN COSTUME MUSEUM
Ruleville

In 1959, at age 20, Luster Bayless hitchhiked from Ruleville to Hollywood, California, and landed a job with a costume company. That position began a lifetime career of designing costumes for some of America's most fabled actors and actresses. Bayless has brought his enormous collection of costumes back to his hometown and now houses them in a restored turn-of-the-century dry goods store. The museum features costumes worn by a Who's Who cast of Hollywood, including John Wayne, with whom Bayless worked closely during much of his career. Located at 104 North Ruby in Ruleville, the museum is open Tuesday-Saturday from 9:30 am to 5 pm—or so. Admission: adults $5.00, senior citizens $3.50, children under 12 are free with an adult. If the museum is closed, walk down to the Hollywood Outpost and someone will give you the tour. (601) 756-2171 or 756-2344.

Costume worn by Marilyn Monroe in Gentlemen Prefer Blonds

THE ETHEL WRIGHT MOHAMED MUSEUM

Belzoni

With intricate, colorful stitches Ethel Wright Mohamed painted stories of her marriage, eight children, and life in the Delta. The museum exhibits an extensive collection of creative stichery by the late Mrs. Mohamed. Her work also appears in the permanent collection of the Smithsonian Institute. By appointment, guests are given a very personal tour by her daughter, Carol Ives. The museum, also known as Mama's Dream World, is located in Mrs. Mohamed's home at 307 Central Street in Belzoni. No admission. (601) 247-1433.

"Waiting for the Stork"

"My Pot of Gold"

THE BOOKER–THOMAS MUSEUM
Lexington

Modest in size but not in content, Fannye Booker's museum offers a glimpse into the past with its eclectic collection of farm tools, family photos, clothing, furniture, a log cabin, and even a preacher's traveling library. Her collection began in the '30s with belongings left behind by black Mississippians migrating north, and has been expanded with the donated possessions of friends and family who have left to meet their Maker. With animated stories of her days as a farmhand, teacher, and boardinghouse owner, the 86-year-old Mrs. Booker gives life and meaning to every artifact. Housed in a small brick building behind Mrs. Booker's house, the museum is located on State Highway 12 west, just outside of Lexington on the north side of the road. Look for a ranch-style brick house with metal wagon wheels bordering the driveway. Admission is free and by appointment. (601) 834-2672.

C.B. "BUDDIE" NEWMAN MUSEUM
Valley Park

The highlight of a visit to C.B. "Buddie" Newman's museum is a mile-long ride on his miniature, air-powered train. Buddie, the former Speaker of the Mississippi House of Representatives, will even let you blow the whistle. The railroad always has been an important part of his life. His father came to Valley Park in 1917 as a Section Manager for the railroad. Buddie was delivered by a railroad doctor in a modest home that is situated a few yards from the railroad. He spent his childhood days riding the rails with his father, swimming under trestles, and putting Coca-Cola bottle caps on the tracks to watch with amazement as passing trains flattened them to slivers.

So in 1985, when the railroad company decided to abandon the line that runs through the family property, he decided to keep a part of it to share his fascination and love for the railroad

with others. He purchased a portion of the track, two railroad cars, and a caboose, and created a museum that features artifacts, photographs, and memorabilia about the railroad, as well as farming, Delta floods, the military, and his 40-year career in the Mississippi legislature.

The museum is behind Newman's home, which is located on U.S. Highway 61 in Valley Park, 21 miles north of Vicksburg. If Buddie is home, he's glad to open his museum, or you can call ahead for an appointment. No admission. (601) 636-0345.

DR. LINDLEY'S VETERINARY MUSEUM
Vicksburg

Lovers of "all creatures great and small" will enjoy a visit with Dr.
William Lindley, Mississippi's James Herriot, who began practicing
veterinary medicine in 1933. In three tin sheds on his property and
several rooms of his home, he has created a personal tribute to his
profession and to the animals to which he has dedicated his working
life. From baboons to armadillos, he pays homage to the animal
world and their scientific contributions to the improvement of
human life. His homemade exhibits teach the history of veterinary
medicine, highlighting the men and women who played major roles
in the development of the profession. Dr. Lindley's keen sense of
humor and seemingly limitless knowledge of veterinary medicine
make for a very informative and entertaining tour.

Dr. Lindley's property is located off Halls Ferry Road in
Vicksburg. Call (601) 636-0964 for an appointment and directions.

AMERICAN HERITAGE "BIG RED" FIRE MUSEUM
Louisville

When W.A. "Bill" Taylor stepped aside to let his children run the family business, he began looking for something to occupy his time. A friend rekindled a childhood interest in fire engines, and Taylor has been collecting and restoring antique firefighting vehicles ever since. Taylor still acts as chairman of the family's two manufacturing companies, but most of his time is spent restoring his growing collection of firefighting apparatus.

Mr. Taylor has a total of 19 engines (seven await restoration). Included in the collection are a horse-drawn bucket brigade unit built in 1797, an early 19th-century hand pumper, an 1888 steam engine, an 1890 horse-drawn aerial ladder truck, an 1929 Ahrens-Fox Pumper, and several hundred pieces of firefighting equipment.

Admission to the private museum is free and by appointment. To arrange a tour, call (601) 773-3421 for Bill Taylor or Michael Cravens. The main museum is located at 332 N. Church Avenue (also known as Business 15) a few blocks north of Main Street.

Courtesy of the American Heritage "Big Red" Fire Museum

An 1888 Steam Engine

JERRY CLOWER'S MUSEUM
Liberty

Jerry Clower is, as the saying goes, "a home boy done good." Jerry grew up in Amite County, played football at Mississippi State, served in the Navy, and then went to work as a fertilizer salesman. A natural storyteller, Jerry became a top salesman and was soon asked to speak to audiences of farmers. The response to his humorous stories of life in rural Mississippi was so great that, with the help of friends, Jerry cut his first album and launched a new career. After 21 albums, four books, and nine consecutive awards for "Country Comic of the Year," Jerry's house overflowed with memorabilia. When the Clowers moved to their new home east of Liberty, they constructed a building to house the collection, which includes his personal photo album, posters, awards, gifts, and keys to a host of cities. The museum is usually shown by the Clowers' staff, but you also may be greeted by Homerline, Jerry's childhood sweetheart and wife, or Jerry himself when he is in town.

Admission to the museum is free and by appointment only. Call Jerry's secretary, Joyce Irwin, at (601) 684-8130 to arrange a tour.

THE PRAYER MUSEUM
Greenwood

Archaeologist Bill Hony is an ardent collector, spending his spare time at estate sales, garage sales, and junk stores, hoping to uncover some valuable piece that the unskilled eyes of others have overlooked. His home contains an interesting collection of antiques, art, 10,000 or so books, and what some might consider junk. After writing a paper on prayer beads, he was inspired to expand his collection to include religious artifacts.

His museum, which is housed in his home, contains pieces from many religions of the world, including: Hinduism, Islam, Buddhism, Balinese, Shinto, American Indian, Judaism, and Christianity. Included among his collection are more than 100 prayer beads from various religions, a church bell, baptismal, and prayer rugs. Bill prizes most: a 1748 book of Catholic sermons from Germany, the Bible of a New York Dutch family that documents the 1813 cholera epidemic, and an 1819 miniature Swedish prayer book. Bill's tour of the museum is very informative and leaves guests with a better understanding of the significance of religion in world history.

Bill Hony's home and museum are located at 611 W. Market Street in Greenwood, 3 blocks west of the courthouse. No admission, but donations are accepted. For an appointment call (601) 453-7306.

PALESTINIAN GARDENS

Lucedale

You don't have to travel very far to see the Holy Land, thanks to Harvell Jackson. The late reverend believed that to truly understand the Bible, people should be familiar with the places that are central to its scriptures. So he and his wife spent years creating their version of the Holy Land on 20 acres in rural George County. Guests can visit Jericho, Bethlehem, Jerusalem, and 20 other cities and sites of the Bible, all of which have been recreated on a miniature scale of one yard per mile. Although the Gardens' lush Mississippi foliage is far from an arid Middle East terrain, it provides a relaxing and peaceful walk through nature.

The Gardens are open March - September, every day from 8 am to 4 pm, and located 12 miles north of Lucedale and 6.5 miles east of U.S. Highway 98. Signs will direct you from Lucedale and from Highway 98. Guests tour the Gardens using printed guide sheets. Tour guides are available by appointment. Admission is $1.50 for adults and 50 cents for children. (601) 947-8422.

WATKINS MUSEUM
Taylorsville

Around 1900 John Watkins moved from Raleigh, where he published the town newspaper, to Taylorsville, a new settlement springing up along the railroad. Mr. Watkins opened a store and founded the *Taylorsville Signal*, which his daughters, Miss Hattie and Miss Marie, continued operating after his death. When the sisters retired in 1962, they put the last issue of the *Signal* to rest. Throughout the paper's life, every issue came off a hand-set, manual press. In 1972, with the help of the Taylorsville Garden Club, the Watkins Museum was created. It's said that the sisters didn't like to throw anything away. The collection in the museum suggests just that. A tribute to the uncommon Watkins sisters, the museum contains the old press, furniture, memorabilia and a collection of newspapers. It is located next to the water tower on Eureka Street. Admission is free and by appointment. Call (601) 785-6531 to arrange a tour.

INTERNATIONAL CHECKER HALL OF FAME

Petal

When Charles Walker was a young man, his sweetheart always kept him waiting before their dates. So he would pass the time away by playing checkers with his future father-in-law. Those games sparked a lifelong passion for checkers that has garnered Walker numerous championship titles and inspired him to create the International Checker Hall of Fame. Walker, a rags-to-riches millionaire, built the checkered palace in 1979 after he discovered there was no monument to his

Courtesy of the Checker Hall of Fame

favorite game. The hall is part of Walker's 30-acre estate. Checker enthusiasts from the United States and many foreign countries come to the hall to vie for championship titles. The hall consists of numerous rooms containing checkers memorabilia and some unrelated pieces, like a knight's suit of armor. The most memorable room is the giant checkers playing arena. Most of the floor is covered with a 16-square-foot regulation checkerboard, surrounded by a second-floor spectators' gallery. During tournaments opponents play on a regular-sized checkerboard while their moves are duplicated for spectators on the giant board, using large pillows resembling checkers. The Hall of Fame is located on Lynn Rae Road in Petal and open by appointment from 9 am to 5 pm Monday - Friday. Admission is free. (601) 582-7090.

The General Store at Country Charm Antiques & Museum

COUNTRY CHARM ANTIQUES & MUSEUM
Eudora

Almost single-handedly, Beth Farnell has re-created the rural America of our ancestors. After retiring from a career in nursing administration in 1979, she decided to open an antique store. She purchased an old farm in Eudora and opened the store in a log cabin on the property. Beth confesses she loves buying and collecting antiques more than selling them, so she soon outgrew the cabin. She moved five more cabins onto the property (one of which was used as a Civil War hospital), and refurbished several existing buildings to house her collection. She now has 12 buildings—each containing early American primitive antiques arranged to depict what rural life might have been like. In the general store there's a pot-bellied stove, checkerboard, cheese cutter, scales, and old jars and tins. The sewing room contains a loom dating to the 1700s, spinning wheels, yarn winders, and a quilting frame. The laundry room holds antique washing machines, washboards, wringers, and irons. Antiques also fill a tool house, smokehouse, hired man's house, schoolhouse/chapel, and barn.

The museum is open "most of the time" from 12 pm to 4 pm Friday, Saturday, and Sunday, and any other time Ms. Farnell is home, as well as by appointment. Admission is $3.00 for adults, and children under 12 are admitted free. To get there from I-55, take the Hernando exit and travel 8.9 miles west on State Highway 304. The museum is on the left and marked by a very small sign. (601) 429-5359.

BEER CONTAINER COLLECTION

D'Iberville

Beer connoisseurs traveling through Mississippi will find Warren Fuller's beer container collection very impressive. Fuller, along with Midge Amryan, has amassed a meticulously organized collection of over 15,000 beer cans, bottles, and related memorabilia. In the two-story building that Fuller bought solely to house the collection, containers are separated into rooms based on their origination in either the U.S. or a foreign country. Over 80 countries, from Lapland to Togo, are represented in his collection of foreign containers. The United States collection includes generic, non-alcoholic, antique and micro-brewery containers. Fuller, a member of Beer Can Collectors of America, began his collection by saving his own and gathering discarded ones, but today he acquires them mostly at trade shows. He enjoys sharing his collection with visitors when he is home. Call ahead for an appointment and directions. Located at 3298 Bay Shore Drive. (601) 392-2150.

CORNER DRUG STORE
Vicksburg

Joe Gerache, owner of the Corner Drug Store, spent his boyhood summers combing the hills of Vicksburg in search of Civil War relics. Today, his vast collection includes Civil War weaponry and projectiles, as well as apothecary and surgical artifacts. Most of his treasures are housed at his drug store, where shelved next to Pepto-Bismol and Band-aids, you might find aging bottles of Dr. Miles New Heart Cure or William Radam's Microbe Killer, which claims it "Cures all Diseases." His collection also includes bullets, the chief anesthetic of Civil War surgeons, scarred with the tooth enamel of some unfortunate infantrymen.

The Corner Drug Store is located at 1123 Washington Street in downtown Vicksburg and open from 8 am - 6 pm, Monday - Saturday, and Sunday from 9 am - 11 am. (601) 636-2756.

JOHN REDMON'S ARROWHEAD COLLECTION

Seminary

In 1967, to help his son add to his arrowhead collection, John Redmon began searching the area's fields and riverbanks in search of these ancient artifacts. It wasn't until he discovered nearly a thousand that he realized it had become his own hobby. His collection now includes between 8,000 and 9,000 arrowheads along with fishhooks, bone needles, beads, cutting devices, and several birds carved of stone. The artifacts date from 8000 B.C to 1200 A.D., when American Indians thrived in Mississippi.

Mr. Redmon and Mary Alma, his wife of 55 years, enjoy sharing the collection with visitors. To get there, take U.S. Highway 49 to Seminary, follow State Highway 590 East through the town, then turn left on State Highway 535 North, go five miles and just before Eminence Baptist Church turn right (a green arrowhead marks the road). The Redmon home is the first brick house on the right, and the collection is housed in a beautiful brick barn Mr. Redmon built himself. No admission. Call (601) 722-3633 for an appointment.

SAM LINDSEY'S MODEL TRAIN COLLECTION

Laurel

Like many 12-year-old boys, Sam Lindsey got a model train for Christmas. Unlike many, Lindsey turned his toy into a lifelong hobby. Now 74, he has 56 model passenger trains depicting the 1940s and 1950s, when riding the rails was at its height. His trains are on display at the Hobby Corner in Laurel, one of three successful businesses he began, and whose sole purpose is the sale and service of model trains. Several trains can run simultaneously on the 400 feet of track displaying the collection. Most uncommon is the "Double Helix," a spiral track that was designed to run trains

up and down the steepest grade possible. Although Mr. Lindsey sold the business to enjoy retirement, he still spends time at the store, and he or the current owner, Allen Strange, will be happy to run the trains for you. The Hobby Corner is located at 1535 N. 1st Avenue in Laurel and open Tuesday, Wednesday, Friday, and Saturday from 9 am to 6 pm, and Thursday from 9 am to 10 pm. (601) 649-4501.

RODNEY
PRESBYTERIAN CHURCH

Chartered in Jan. 1828, as the
Presbyterian Church of Petit
Gulf. Shelled by the gunboat
"Rattler" when Federal sailors
were captured by Confederate
cavalry while attending Sunday
services, September 13, 1863

RODNEY

A handful of residents and occasional deer camp inhabitants keep Rodney from becoming a ghost town. Selected for its prime location, the area was settled in 1722 on the high banks of the Mississippi River. Nearly 100 years later Rodney officially became a town. By the 1840s and 1850s, known as the golden age of steamboating, the town had become a business and cultural center. The bustling river town had two banks, two newspapers, a large hotel with a huge ballroom, several churches, the first opera house in the state, and several saloons and gambling houses. In 1852 a fire destroyed much of the town, the first of several blows that led to Rodney's descent to the near ghost town it is today. Rodney rebuilt, and by 1860, with a population of 4,000, was one of Mississippi's largest and most prosperous cities.

Then, during the Civil War, a Union gunboat shelled the town after Confederate cavalrymen captured a group of Union seamen attending services at the Presbyterian Church. A cannonball is still lodged in the front of the church. Although Rodney escaped with this single battle scar, the town and surrounding plantations were depleted of their wealth at war's end.

Nature, however, was more merciless. The river changed its course and left the town high and dry. In 1869 a second disastrous fire destroyed much of the town, and then the railroad passed it by. With the exception of a barking dog or two, Rodney is today hauntingly quiet. A cotton field now thrives in the old riverbed. Two churches, a saloon, Masonic lodge, and old store still stubbornly stand. Up the steep hill behind the Presbyterian Church, you'll find the town cemetery, filled with overgrown family gravesites surrounded by ornate wrought-iron fences, a sign of Rodney's more prosperous days. Visitors with a vivid imagination will enjoy Rodney, easily conjuring up images of life in this once colorful and prosperous river town.

Going south on U.S. Highway 61, take the right at the south side of the Lorman Country Store, go to the stop sign and turn left, bear to the right at the fork, and after several miles you'll reach Rodney.

ROCKY SPRINGS

Since the 1790s Rocky Springs, located 17 miles northeast of Natchez, has been a popular place to stop along the Natchez Trace. In the early days travelers spent the night at Rocky Spring's notorious Red House Inn, said to be the place where bandits sized up travelers and chose their victims. Despite risking such encounters, many travelers were attracted to the area's fertile land and numerous springs.

By 1860, Rocky Springs had grown into a thriving town with a population of 2,616. It boasted at least two stores, a church, a bakery, post office, Masonic lodge, schools, several artisans' shops, and numerous large homes. But between 1860 and 1920 the area was devastated by the Civil War, yellow fever, the boll weevil, and severe land erosion. The town of Rocky Springs finally died in the 1930s.

Today, Rocky Springs is still a popular rest stop on the Natchez Trace. Visitors can walk a short nature trail that winds through the old town site, where two rusting safes and several abandoned cisterns remain. The Methodist Church, which was built in 1837, still overlooks the old town site and is open to the public during the day. Behind the church lies the town's graveyard, surrounded by old trees dripping with Spanish moss.

Visitors can also hike on the Old Natchez Trace, wade in the shallow waters of the Little Sand Creek, and camp for free at the primitive campsites.

GRAND GULF

Grand Gulf was named for an eddy, or gulf, that was created where the Big Black River empties into the Mississippi River. The area was settled by the French in the early 1700s, but Grand Gulf was an unimportant outpost until the cotton planters discovered its advantageous shipping location in the early 1800s. The town quickly grew into a prosperous commerce center. In one week in 1836 there were 35 steamboats that put into the dock, making it one of the busiest ports between New Orleans and St. Louis. Two newspapers, a bank, a hospital, a school, churches, and numerous stores and businesses served the population of about 1,000.

Then a series of disasters began that would eventually destroy the town. First, a steamer exploded at the dock, starting fires that burned for days, consuming a large section of the town. Next, a yellow fever epidemic claimed the lives of many citizens. Then, a tornado ripped through the center of town. The Mississippi River dealt the cruelest blow in the late 1850s when it devoured 55 city blocks. By 1860 the population had dropped to a dismal 158. During the Civil War, Fort Coburn and Fort Wade overlooked what was left of the town, and after the ultimate fall of the forts, the Yankees burned what remained.

Grand Gulf Military Monument Park was created to preserve the memory of the town and the battle that occurred there. The park includes Fort Coburn, Fort Wade, Grand Gulf Cemetery, a museum, campgrounds, picnic areas, hiking trails, an observation tower, and several restored buildings. The park is located 10 miles northwest of Port Gibson and U.S. Highway 61 on the picturesque Grand Gulf Road. Admission to the park is free, but a nominal fee is charged to tour the museum and for RV camping. (601) 437-5911.

Courtesy of the Department of Economic & Community Development

Interior of the Old Country Store at Lorman

COUNTRY STORES

Country stores were once the heart of rural communities. Today, only a few grand country stores remain on the backroads of Mississippi. Although they are no longer the place to buy all of life's necessities, friendly hellos and good conversation are still plentiful. A visit to one of Mississippi's country stores takes you back to a simpler and slower pace of life.

LORMAN COUNTRY STORE

Eleven miles south of Port Gibson on U.S. Highway 61; present building dates to 1890; features museum; open Monday through Saturday from 8 am to 6 pm, and Sundays from noon to 6 pm; visitors can get directions to the old town of Rodney and other interesting sites in the area.

Courtesy of Jack E Davis

WAGNER'S

Located in Church Hill on State Highway 553; 13 miles north of Natchez and across from an imposing antebellum Episcopal Church; the store was built prior to 1870; open 8:30 am - 7 pm, Monday - Saturday.

Inside the Pond Store

POND STORE

Fourteen miles west of Woodville on the Pond-Pinckneyville Road; built in 1881; open 7 am to 7 pm seven days a week; the entrance to Clark Creek Natural Area, one of Mississippi's unique and beautiful natural treasures, is located near the store.

BRYAN'S GROCERY

Located southeast of Carthage; take State Highway 35 south to State Highway 488 and drive a few miles to the Freeny Community; present store built in 1929 through a community effort after a fire destroyed the original structure; owner Rose Bryan has pine needle baskets, split white-oak baskets, and hundreds of Choctaw Indian baskets for sale; open 6 am to 6 pm, Monday - Saturday.

H.D. GIBBES AND SON GENERAL STORE

Opened in 1900; located in Learned off State Highway 18 in southwest Hinds County; features collection of the stores original fixtures and equipment; serves hamburgers; open Monday - Saturday, 7 am to 7:30 pm or around sundown.

BIGBEE VALLEY GENERAL STORE

Located on State Highway 388 in Noxubee County near the Alabama state line; store was rebuilt in 1923 after it burned; community post office still operates in the store; open from 6:30 am to 5 pm Monday, Tuesday, Wednesday and Friday, closes at noon on Thursday and 2 pm on Saturday.

ONWARD STORE

Located on U.S. Highway 61, 25 miles north of Vicksburg; built in 1913. The store is located near the site where President Theodore Roosevelt, while on a hunt in November 1902, refused to shoot a captured bear. That incident gave birth to the "Teddy Bear." The store displays photographs documenting the hunt. The store also serves good burgers. Open 7:30 am to 7:30 pm seven days a week.

Courtesy of Causeyville General Store

CAUSEYVILLE GENERAL STORE

Located on State Highway 19 south of Meridian; built in 1895; features musical museum with player pianos; a grist mill grinds corn on Saturday. Open 7 am - 7 pm, Monday - Saturday and 1 pm to 5 pm on Sunday.

VIRILLIA STORE

Located northwest of Canton; take Interstate 55 to the Canton exit and go west until you reach the old gin at Virillia Road and go 3.5 miles north on the road; store records date to 1869; store hours vary with crop harvesting, but they are generally open "from can to can't."

SCIPLE GRIST MILL
Kemper County

In 1830, when the Sciples purchased a water mill and began a family business, it's doubtful they realized that five generations would follow in their footsteps. But Edward and Eva Grace Sciple and their children will carry the tradition into the next century. Located in rural Kemper County, the mill was built in 1790 and owned by several families prior to being purchased by the Sciples. Until the mid '50s (that's the 1950s), the mill ginned cotton and sawed lumber. Today it grinds wheat and corn. A visit to the mill will carry you back to the last century, to a slow and uncomplicated time. To get there, take State Highway 39 North and follow the signs. The mill operates Monday - Friday, 7 am - 3 pm, and Saturday from 7 am to 12 pm, accept during deer (gun) season; the November-January schedule varies annually. (601) 743-2295.

Edward Sciple in his mill.

COBB'S SORGHUM MILL

Sardis

Pancakes a little dry? Then a visit to the farm of third-generation
syrup makers, Royce and Sandra Cobb, is suggested. There you can
purchase Mississippi cane syrup and learn about the labor-intensive
process of making this sweet, southern delicacy.   Late August to
September is "cooking time," when an electric mill squeezes the juice
from home-grown cane. Then the juice is steam-cooked into a thick-
flowing syrup. It takes seven to eight gallons of juice to make just
one gallon of syrup. Travelers are welcome to stop and look at the
operation and buy syrup any time of the year. The cost for syrup is
$3.50 for a pint and $9.00 for a four-pound can. The Cobb's Farm is
located halfway between Sardis and Batesville. If traveling on U.S.
Highway 51, turn at the Cobb's Sorghum Mill sign and drive one
mile on the gravel road; from Interstate 55 take the Batesville exit to
Highway 51 and go north until you see the sign. (601) 487-1088.
Each fall syrup is also made at McCall Creek west of Brookhaven, at
House, west of Carthage, and at French Camp on the Natchez Trace.

Courtesy of Cobb's Sorghum Mill

SUNSHINE FARMS
Noxubee County

If you're looking for an entertaining and educational family outing, make a trip to Sunshine Farms. Guests can take a 1/2 to 1 1/2 hour tour of this working farm, where they can pet or feed hundreds of animals, including miniature horses, sheep, cows, pigs, rabbits, chickens, ducks, swans, skunks, turkeys, and a donkey. Children can take a memorable ride on a miniature horse, which stands at or below 34 inches from the last mane hair to the ground.

The farm tour changes with the seasons. In the fall guests are treated to a hayride to a nearby field, where they can pick cotton or a pumpkin to take home. The spring brings many new baby animals to the farm, and guests can hold the kittens, puppies, bunnies, and chicks.

Sunshine Farms is open Monday through Saturday from 9 am to 5 pm. Guests can bring a lunch and picnic under nearby trees. To get there take U.S. Highway 45, turn east on Prairie Point Road (just outside of Macon) and drive 5 miles, turn left at the Sunshine Farms sign and go 1 mile. The cost is $3.50 per person plus tax, and children under two years old are admitted free. Corn for feeding is available for 25 cents. Tour groups are welcome. (601) 726-2264.

Curious sheep at Sunshine Farms

OLD ORDER GERMAN BAPTIST COMMUNITY
Covington County

Fifty years ago, milking a cow, churning butter, making your own soap, or living without electricity wasn't out of the ordinary in Mississippi. But to see that self-reliant lifestyle today is like stepping back to generations past. That's what makes a trip to the small Old Order German Baptist community outside of Mt. Olive so interesting. There you'll find three farms owned by William Diehl and his family, who moved to Mississippi in the lates 1970s in search of unspoiled rural land and a good place to raise a family.

Each home offers something interesting. At William Diehl's you can purchase delicious made-to-order baked goods or have your furniture upholstered. At the home of Robert Jamison you can pick

berries, muscadines, and peaches when in season; purchase beautiful baskets made by 17-year-old Roger; and buy hand-sewn quilts, home-churned butter, and homemade soap from Mrs. Jamison. And then, at the home of Bill Diehl you can purchase or order hand-crafted furniture.

The German Baptist lifestyle and dress is similar to the Amish or Mennonites. They rely on the bounty of the earth, growing or raising nearly everything they eat, and making from scratch much of what they use. For transportation they depend primarily on horse and buggies, bicycles, and their feet. It's a "simple and contented lifestyle," as the Jamisons themselves describe it, that in today's hectic world, many visitors will find appealing.

To get there take U.S. Highway 49 to the State Highway 35 North exit, near Mt. Olive, and go one mile to State Highway 532 east. Bill Diehl's home is 1.7 miles down Highway 532; William Diehl's home is 7.3 miles from the 532 turn-off; to reach Robert Jamison's home turn right at William Diehl's and drive 4/10 of 1 mile. The mailing address for all three families is Route 1, Mt. Olive, MS 39119.

BATSON'S LOG HOME & FISH FARM

Wiggins

When he was a teenager, 92-year old Hollis Batson admired the land near his family home where a natural spring bubbled up from the earth. After he married and began raising his family, the property went on the market and he bought it in 1928. From timber on the property and from old logs pulled from nearby Red Creek, he built a sturdy log cabin with a porch encircling the home. He finished the interior with panels of magnolia, cherry, oak, and poplar wood. The guests who came to their house-warming party in 1936 signed a dining room wall, and those faded signatures are still there today.

Soon after the log cabin was constructed, he built a dam and created a waterwheel to pump the springwater to the house. When he began moving the dirt, he found that others had gravitated to and relied on the spring long before. There he found Indian arrowheads and other artifacts. He also unearthed a strongbox in a dugout room, which the notorious Copeland Gang, who terrorized south Mississippi in the 1840s and 1850s, reputedly used as a hide-out.

Today, Archie Batson, the youngest of the eight Batson chidren, has harnessed the pure springwater to raise catfish and crawfish commercially. On land adjacent to the cabin, he has numerous ponds, some of which are open to the public to fish for catfish, bass, bream, and even rainbow trout. The trout pond was created naturally by beaver dams near the origin of the spring. The fish thrive in this cool springwater and it is so clear that you can even see them biting your hook. Guests can also camp primitive-style on Red Creek among the goats and ponies that roam the property.

To fish in the ponds or camp, call Archie Batson at (601) 928-5271. To arrange to see the Batson waterwheel and log cabin, call Mr. Batson's daughter, Mary Elaine Wesson, at (601) 928-2310. To get there take U.S. Highway 49 to Wiggins and take the State Highway 26 exit, then head west toward Poplarville. The property is a couple of miles from the interstate and is marked by signs. Donations are accepted for touring the home and the waterwheel.

TRAPPER'S GATOR FARM

Jones County

After 30 years of professional trapping in south Mississippi, Wayne Parker has become known in those parts simply as Trapper. He's always had a natural liking for the animal kingdom, surrounding himself with everything from canaries to alligators. A few years ago he and his wife, Linda, decided to open their growing collection of animals to the public. The farm's residents include deer, goats, snakes, birds, foxes, bobcats, a cougar, and over 30 alligators. Dinnertime at the gator pond is a captivating sight. A swarm of gators are lured to the edge of the pond by the sound of Trapper chopping whole chickens on a wood block. These fearless-looking reptiles quickly devour their meal in a feeding frenzy. But there's also a more gentle side to the farm. At the petting barn, children can touch fawns, turtles, and guinea pigs. Many animals on the farm were injured, orphaned, or given to Trapper because people knew he would give them a good home.

Trapper's Gator Farm is located in the Landrum Community, east of Laurel. From I-59 take the State Highway 15 South exit and follow the signs. Open 5-7:30 pm weekdays, 10 to 7:30 pm Saturdays, and 12:30 - 6 pm Sundays. Admission is $2.00 for adults and $1.00 for children. (601) 428-4967.

Dinnertime at Trapper's Gator Farm

WATERMELON FESTIVAL
Mize

Held every July, the Watermelon Festival features watermelon-eating and seed-spitting contests; a greased watermelon race; largest watermelon contest; arts and crafts; live country and gospel music; and, of course, the crowning of the Watermelon Queen. (601) 733-5478.

Courtesy of The Belzoni Banner

Catfish-eating contest

WORLD CATFISH FESTIVAL
Belzoni

The self-proclaimed "catfish capital" pays homage to its favorite fish with a festival each April. The one-day event is filled with entertainment, arts and crafts, a catfish-eating contest, and free tours of the spring flowers at Wister Gardens. One of the festival's highlights is the crowning of the World Catfish Queen. (601) 247-4838.

NATIONAL SWEET POTATO FESTIVAL
Vardaman

The town of Vardaman honors the sweet potato, the backbone of the area's economy, with a festival every November. The week of activities include a sweet potato pie-eating contest; a contest for the best washed and waxed bushel of sweet potatoes; a sweet potato cooking contest; a flea market and arts and crafts show; and the crowning of the Sweet Potato Queen. (601) 628-6833.

NESHOBA COUNTY FAIR
Neshoba County

In 1889 Mississippians came to the Neshoba County Fair in wagons, then pitched tents and camped for a week of festivities. Today, as the oldest remaining campground fair in the U.S., that tradition continues when more than 500 rustic cabins fill with kinfolk and friends, gathered to share in fellowship amidst the week's events, including: horse races, country and western bands, carnival rides, a beauty pageant, southern food, and a constant stream of political orators. The fair is generally held the first week of August, nine miles southwest of Philadelphia. Phone (601) 656-1742.

FIRST MONDAY TRADE DAY
Ripley

Need a hunting dog, chicken, generator, or sunshades? You can find that and much more at the First Monday Trade Day. The event originated in 1893 when local residents gathered on the Courthouse Square to sell or barter anything they had a notion to offer. Today, hundreds of vendors gather to peddle more than you can imagine— providing hours of intrigue and entertainment. Located on Highway 15 south of Ripley, First Monday Trade Day is held monthly beginning on the preceding Saturday, peaking on Sunday, and winding down on Monday. Free admission. (601) 837-4051.

CHIMNEYVILLE CRAFT FESTIVAL
Jackson

Over 100 of the South's finest craftsmen gather the first weekend of December at the Mississippi Trade Mart in Jackson to show their wares. Artists exhibit baskets, jewelry, weaving, pottery, wood carvings, hand-blown glass, and more at this exceptional event. $3.00 admission. The event is sponsored by the Craftsmen's Guild of Mississippi, which operates two craft stores year round, one on the Natchez Trace at Ridgeland and the other at the Agriculture and Forestry Museum on Lakeland Drive in Jackson. (601) 981-0019.

Courtesy of Craftsmen's Guild of Mississippi, Inc.

*Shopping for Walter Anderson prints at
the Chimneyville Crafts Festival*

DIXIE NATIONAL LIVESTOCK SHOW, RODEO, and WESTERN FESTIVAL
Jackson

The Dixie National boasts the largest livestock show east of the Mississippi. Over 50,000 people attend nearly three weeks of events, which include Arabian horse shows to lamb shows and everything in between, local and national entertainment, dances, a parade, armadillo races, and a rodeo that will keep you on the edge of your seat. Festivities generally begin the end of January. (601) 961-4000.

MISSISSIPPI STATE FAIR
Jackson

The Mississippi State Fair is held for two weeks each October at the State Fairgrounds, just a stone's throw from downtown Jackson. Traditional competitions for livestock, arts and crafts, and food are held, but the event is far from being a quiet country fair. Thousands of people flock to the midway for the thrill of the rides and to sample the tempting enjoy-now-pay-later food. The pot-bellied pig races are a must to see. Admission charged. (601) 961-4000.

CANTON FLEA MARKET
Canton

Just after sunrise twice a year all roads leading to the small town of Canton begin to swell with buses and cars loaded with bargain hunters from near and far. They come with money in hand to purchase arts and crafts from over 1,000 exhibitors from 26 states whose booths fill the Canton courthouse square and surrounding blocks. The event is held the second Thursday in May and the second Thursday in October. Wear your most comfortable walking shoes. No admission. (601) 859-1606.

JACKSON STATE HOMECOMING PARADE
Jackson

Loyal alumni of Jackson State, Mississippi's largest historically black university, come from all corners of the nation to celebrate homecoming each year. One of the highlights of the weekend's festivities is the parade, which features a host of bands from as far away as Chicago, Detroit, and Oklahoma City. Thousands of people line the streets of downtown Jackson while marching bands, dancers, beauty queens of all ages, ROTC squadrons, and more participate in what is probably the state's biggest and most entertaining parade. (601) 968-2272.

MAP OF RESTAURANTS

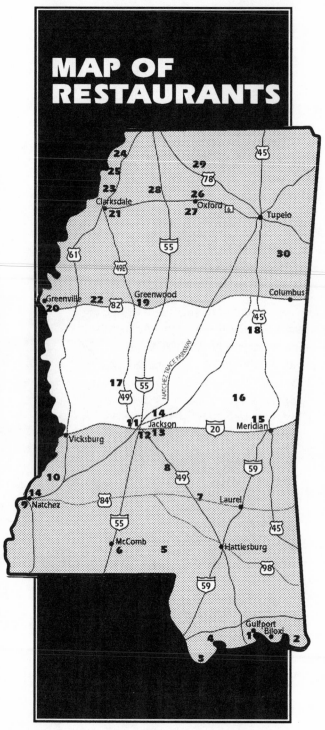

SOUTH

1 Blow Fly Inn, Gulfport
2 Jocelyn's, Ocean Springs
3 Jack's, Waveland
4 Ruth's Bakery,
   Bay St. Louis
5 Leatha's Bar-B-Q,
   Foxworth
6 The Dinner Bell,
   McComb
7 The Country Kitchen,
   Collins
8 Revolving Tables,
   Mendenhall
9 King's Tavern, Natchez
10 JB's Place, Port Gibson

CENTRAL

11 The Mayflower, Jackson
12 Hal & Mal's, Jackson
13 Primos Cafe, Jackson
14 Cock of the Walk,
   Natchez and Jackson
15 Weidmann's, Meridian
16 Peggy's, Philadelphia
17 K.O.K., Yazoo City
18 The Ole Country
   Bakery, Brooksville

NORTH

19 Lusco's, Greenwood
20 Doe's Eat Place,
   Greenville
21 Chamoun's Rest Haven,
   Clarksdale
22 The Crown Restaurant,
   Indianola
23 Uncle Henry's Place,
   Moon Lake
24 The Hollywood,
   Robinsonville
25 The Blue & White,
   Tunica
26 Smitty's, Oxford
27 Taylor Grocery & Restaurant,
   Taylor
28 Como Steak House, Como
29 Phillips Grocery,
   Holly Springs
30 Bill's Hamburgers, Amory

RESTAURANTS

The restaurants featured in this guide aren't the fanciest in the state, but they're usually where you'll find the locals eating delicious food at reasonable prices. These restaurants have good food and character to match, like Peggy's in Philadelphia, where for 30 years she has trusted her customers to leave their money in a basket on the way out the door. Each in their own way, these restaurants celebrate Mississippi's culture as well as its cuisine.

Sign beckoning customers to Taylor Grocery & Restaurant

BLOW FLY INN
Gulfport

For 30 years now locals have "swarmed" to the Blow Fly Inn to feast on the restaurant's tasty barbecued ribs, hearty steaks, and fresh seafood—all seasoned with a sense of humor. The curious name started as a joke and then stuck. The phone company didn't find it quite so humorous, however, and for two years refused to list the name in the directory. Today, the restaurant honors the origin of its name by garnishing each plate with a black plastic fly.

While dining at this dockside restaurant, you can watch the mullet jump as the sun sets over Bayou Bernard, and may even catch inquisitive alligators spying on you from the dock's edge. Inside, the decor is simple and time-worn. Year round, white Christmas lights framing the windows illuminate aging wallpaper decorated with sailing ships.

The Blow Fly Inn is open Monday - Friday from 3 pm to 11 pm, Saturday from 10 am to 11 pm, and closed on Sunday. The restaurant is accessible by boat or land. To get there by land, take U.S. Highway 49 (or 25th Avenue) to Pass Road and go west, drive north on Washington Avenue until it dead-ends and you will reach Bayou Bernard and the restaurant. (601) 896-9812.

JOCELYN'S
Ocean Springs

It was to the benefit of restaurant-goers when 11 years ago Jocelyn Mayfield decided to strike out on her own. For years she had worked for one of the finer restaurants on the coast. So, with the help of her husband, she transformed his parents' modest home into a restaurant, painted it an eye-catching fuschia pink, and inside, created an atmosphere of casual elegance. Jocelyn's serves sophisticated dishes of seafood, beef, and chicken that are pleasing to the eye and palate alike. Save room for a piece of her homemade peanut butter, banana split, or pecan pie. Jocelyn's is located on U.S. 90 East, opposite Eastover Bank in Ocean Springs, and open Monday through Saturday, 5 pm to 10 pm. Cash only. (601) 875-1925.

JACK'S
Waveland

Jack's is a small-town, close-knit kind of place where after a few visits you'll probably be called by name, and for the truly loyal, even have dishes named after you. Housed in a refurbished shotgun house, with creaky floors, a modest decor, and friendly service, Jack's provides an unpretentious and easygoing atmosphere. Fresh-from-the-gulf seafood is brought in by the restaurant's own personal fisherman, who can be seen in the kitchen filleting his catch. Dishes like Christine's Shrimp Bienville, Joe's Oysters Bordelaise, and

Conrad's Swiss Baked Crabmeat have earned Jack's a faithful following. Steaks are also served.

Jack's is located at 324 Coleman Avenue in Waveland and open seven days a week from 5 pm to 9:30 pm. Reservations are suggested for weekends. (601)467-3065.

RUTH'S BAKERY
Bay St. Louis

Ruth's Bakery is a favorite gathering place for citizens of Bay St. Louis. Personal coffee cups of loyal customers hang on the walls and are filled regularly with what some say is the best coffee in town. Each morning locals occupy the scattered tables to read the morning paper and chat about politics, sports, and the town gossip. Antiques fill an adjacent room, and a portion of their sales benefit the Hancock County Historical Society, which owner Ruth Thompson presides over as president. Bay St. Louis is a charming town filled with beautiful old homes and buildings, antiques, art, and fine crafts. Ruth's Bakery is the perfect place to start a one-mile walking tour of the historic "Old Town" section which you can take by following the blue sailboats painted on the sidewalks.

The bakery is located at 130 Court Street and open from 7 am to 5 pm Tuesday through Saturday and on Sundays from 7 am to noon. (601) 467-8201.

LEATHA'S BAR-B-Q INN
Foxworth

Leatha Jackson is a woman of faith—a faith strong enough to deliver her from a life of hard times to one of much-deserved prosperity. One of 14 children, she began earning her keep at age five by picking cotton. She now reigns as the "Stately Matriarch of Mississippi Bar-B-Q." Leatha says she puts God first in everything she does, and when you taste her ribs you'll think they are divinely inspired. A little-known culinary treasure, Leatha's Bar-B-Q Inn serves with each plate of ribs generous portions of delicious coleslaw, real fried potatoes, and mammoth glasses of iced tea. Hefty chunks of moist and succulent meat practically fall from the bone of the ribs, which are covered in Leatha's secret sauce, only once, before cooking slowly for five to six hours.

Leatha's is a family business, with sisters, sons, daughters-in-law, grandchildren, and cousins, cooking, cleaning, and waiting on tables. At Leatha's it's the food and service that count, not the decor. Diners are seated at vinyl-covered tables with mismatched chairs, plates, and serving utensils. Leatha frequently visits the dining room to make sure customers are satisfied. She runs her business by a simple but sensible motto: "If the customers are pleased...I'm pleased! If the customers are not pleased...I want to know so I can please you!"

The restaurant is so far off the beaten path that a map is helpful. Follow the map to Foxworth, and when you cross the railroad tracks, inhale deeply and follow your nose to a dinner of world class bar-b-q.

Leatha's is open Thursday through Saturday from 11:30 am to 11:00 pm. Cash only. (601) 736-5163.

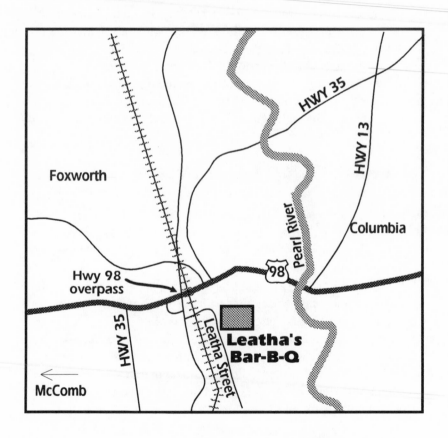

THE DINNER BELL
McComb

The Dinner Bell has a reputation for serving simple-but-good southern cooking, and lots of it. Diners are seated at huge round tables where your favorite dish comes with the spin of the lazy Susan. Your choices may include field peas, squash, butterbeans, fresh-sliced tomatoes, ham, chicken-n-dumplings, fried chicken, biscuits, corn bread, and several choices for dessert. The price of a meal ranges from $7 to $8.50, depending on the day you dine. Lunch is served from 11 am to 2 pm, Tuesday - Sunday. Closed Monday. From April through September evening meals are served from 5:30 pm - 8 pm on Friday and Saturday. The restaurant is housed in a colonial-style structure at 229 Fifth Avenue. (601) 684-4883.

THE COUNTRY KITCHEN
Collins

On US-49, just south of Collins, you'll find the Country Kitchen, which doubles as the home of Johnie Rose Pipkins. Guests enter through the side door of her home leading into the kitchen, pick up a plate, and help themselves to pots of southern vittles on her stove and counters. Ms. Pipkins doesn't have a set menu, she just serves "whatever she has a notion to cook that day." But you can count on probably having traditional southern favorites like peas, cornbread, sweet potatoes, and banana pudding. Diners are seated in folding chairs in two rooms of the ranch-style house, and when they want seconds, they just make another trip to the kitchen. The restaurant is open Sunday - Thursday from 11 am - 2 pm. (601) 756- 6211.

REVOLVING TABLES
Mendenhall

In 1915 Mrs. Annie Heil began serving quick, hot, all-you-can-eat meals to train passengers stopping in Mendenhall on their way to destinations north and south. She seated diners at large, round tables with lazy Susans covered with great platters of chicken-n-dumplings, sweet potatoes, butterbeans, cornbread, and other southern delicacies. Today, Mrs. Heil's descendants continue that traditional serving style. Diners need not be shy about spinning the lazy Susan to fill their plate several times with their favorite dish.

Take a hint from the house motto: "Eat 'til it ouches." Located on Old Highway 49 in Mendenhall. The price of a meal is about $10. Open Monday - Saturday from 11 am - 2 pm and for supper from 6 - 7:30 pm, Sunday lunch only from 11 am - 2 pm. (601) 847-3113.

THE MAYFLOWER
Jackson

Dining at the Mayflower makes you feel like you're on the set of an old black-and white movie. Its nostalgia, along with consistently good food, has contributed to the cafe's longevity. The Mayflower opened in 1935 in the midst of the Great Depression and has seen Jackson through boom, bust, and flood. Through it all, the restaurant has served good food at reasonable prices, earning a diverse and loyal clientele. The menu features hearty breakfasts, blue-plate-special lunches, and fresh seafood, all of which will be served at any hour. The Mayflower is open Monday-Thursday from 7:30 am to 10:30 pm and until midnight on Friday and Saturday. BYOB Located at 123 West Capitol Street in Jackson. (601) 355-4122.

HAL & MAL'S
Jackson

If there's a party in Jackson, it usually begins or ends at Hal & Mal's. The establishment is more than a restaurant and bar; it serves as a center of cultural, musical, and festive events for the state's biggest small town. Each week, Hal & Mal's offers an eclectic mix of music, including blues, Celtic, country, and rock 'n' roll. In March, Mal's St. Paddy's Day Parade attracts thousands to downtown Jackson and to the restaurant. Malcolm White is the "idea man" for the business, and also the creator of the St. Patrick's Day parade and many other Jackson events, while brother Hal tends to the restaurant. The menu is as diverse as the music, offering gumbo, tamales, and burgers, as well as specials each evening that always include several seafood dishes. This quasi-cosmopolitan restaurant is where the pulse of Jackson can be taken.

Hal & Mal's is located in a restored warehouse at 200 South Commerce Street in downtown Jackson and serves lunch and dinner Monday - Sunday from 4 pm to 10 pm. The bar closes at around 1 am, depending on the crowd. (601) 948-0888.

PRIMOS CAFE
Jackson

It's been said that the one thing you can always count on is change, but at Primos that's not true. The restaurant opened in 1948 and hasn't changed a thing since, not even the wallpaper. Diners who occupy the red and white vinyl booths each day find the changeless, nostalgic atmosphere both comforting and charming.

Loyal breakfast patrons of Primos Cafe claim the restaurant has the best grits in the state, and in Mississippi that's saying a lot. Primos substitutes half-and-half cream for water, which creates creamy, rich servings of the South's beloved dish. At lunch, the restaurant serves popular blue-plate-special lunches, and on Fridays donut pudding is free for the asking. Seafood and steaks are popular evening meals.

Primos Cafe should not be confused with Primos Northgate, which is located several miles north. The cafe is located at 1016 North State Street, just north of Fortification Street, and opens at 7 am on weekdays and Saturdays, 8 am on Sundays, and closes at 9 pm each evening. (601) 948-4343.

COCK OF THE WALK
Natchez and Jackson

The Cock of the Walk takes its name from the toughest of the brawling, brawny boatmen who traveled the Mississippi in the 19th-century peddling their wares and making mischief at every port city, including Natchez. The mightiest man aboard each boat was called the "Cock of the Walk," recognizable as the undisputed ruler of the roost by the turkey feather proudly brandished from his hat.

The restaurant derived its name and character from those colorful boatmen. Attentive waiters, dressed in the clothing of river men, complete with hat and scarlet turkey feather, serve drinks in metal cups and meals on roughcast dinnerware. Waiters add a moment of suspense and entertainment to the dinner when they flip cornbread from a skillet. The house specialty is fried-to-perfection catfish fillets, served with cornbread, french fries, cole slaw, and pickled onions. Other entrees of catfish, chicken, and shrimp are available, as well as side dishes of fried dill pickles, fried onion rings, and a "pot-o-greens."

Restaurants are located "on-the-bluff" in Natchez at 200 N. Broadway, (601) 446-8920, and in Jackson at the Ross Barnett Reservoir, (601) 856-5500.

KING'S TAVERN
Natchez

Built before 1798, King's Tavern is one of the oldest known buildings dating back to the days of the Natchez Territory. The tavern once offered food and lodging to weary travelers on the Mississippi River and Natchez Trace, and if the walls of King's Tavern could speak, they could tell the personal stories of the people who tamed the Natchez wilderness.

In 1976 the walls did just that. During renovations, a skeleton of a woman with a dagger in her chest was found behind a bricked-up wall. Legend has it that a young maiden named Madeline became the mistress of her employer, Prosper King, the original owner of the tavern. Madeline disappeared while walking home from work one night, and she was never seen again. King's wife is thought to have killed her in a jealous rage. Today, local lore claims that Madeline's ghost roams the tavern, playing pranks on employees and guests.

King's Tavern offers more than ghost stories, though. The restaurant's specialty is prime rib cooked on an outside grill over hickory. Besides beef, shrimp and catfish dishes are also offered.

Today's travelers looking for a unique place to spend the night can stay in the tavern's upstairs suite (while perhaps sharing it with Madeline) above the restaurant. After the restaurant closes, the staff departs, leaving the guests on their own. In the morning guests are treated to breakfast at the Natchez Eola Hotel. King's Tavern is located at 619 Jefferson Street in Natchez and open 5 pm - 10 pm, seven days a week. Entrees begin at $12.00. For information call (601) 446-8845.

JB'S PLACE
Port Gibson

Jessie and Bernice Davis, owners of JB's Place, have a partnership that works. Jessie grows vegetables for the restaurant and tends to business details, while Bernice oversees the kitchen and takes care of customers. JB's has a diverse menu, but is best known for serving soul-satisfying blue-plate-special lunches of their home-grown vegetables, along with pork chops, barbecued chicken, pepper steak, chicken and dressing, and on Saturdays, boiled or fried chitlins. JB's menu also includes traditional southern breakfasts, sandwiches, steaks, and fried catfish.

The restaurant is open from 7:30 am - 2 pm and 5 pm to about 7:30 pm, Monday through Saturday. Closed Sunday. Located at 313 Market Street in Port Gibson, which is one block north of the traffic circle in front of the courthouse. (601) 437-3429.

WEIDMANN'S
Meridian

Weidmann's was established in 1870 when Swiss immigrant Felix Weidmann began serving vegetables and fruits from a counter with four stools. Nurtured through the years by five generations, Weidmann's has become a culinary landmark. The venerable restaurant is in a league of its own, adding to Mississippi history with every piece of Black Bottom Pie served. The menu is enormous. You could probably dine at Weidmann's every day for a year and still have selections left to try. Aging photographs of war heroes, movie stars, and southern beauty queens cover the walls, along with dusty mounted game and a grand old cuckoo clock. Weidmann's record of success can probably be attributed to their motto, "It's the food that counts"—and it does. Weidmann's is located at 210 22nd Avenue in Meridian and open seven days a week from 6 am to 10 pm. (601) 693-1751.

PEGGY'S
Philadelphia

Going to Peggy's for lunch is like sitting down at your grandmother's table. For 33 years Peggy has served wholesome southern-style meals from her home at the corner of Byrd Avenue and Bay Street. The food is served buffet-style from a board nailed between the walls of the hallway connecting the kitchen to the dining room, where guests are seated community-style. The all-you-can-eat buffet includes daily entrees of ham, chicken-n-dumplings, beef tips, pork chops, and fried chicken. On "fried chicken days" Peggy serves as many as 200 people. To-go lunches are available and picked up at the back door of the kitchen.

Aside from the immensely satisfying meal, Peggy's is distinctive because of her pay policy. Years ago when her lunches went from 78 cents to $1.00, it was easier to just let customers leave the money in a basket on the way out the door. She found that people liked to be trusted, and although the price of a meal has increased to $4.50, she has maintained her unique policy.

Lunch is served weekdays from 10:30 am - 2 pm, or until the food runs out. Peggy's is open year round, except Christmas and the week of the Neshoba County Fair.

K.O.K. (or Kit's Oriental Kitchen)
Yazoo City

If you're weary of grits and fried chicken, you should make a trip to K.O.K. Owner and cook Kit Davis serves exceptional dishes of traditional Thai food like Phat Thai and Chicken Curry, as well as standard American fare. With her home-grown herbs and distinctive sauces, Kit will treat you to "an evening that is all for you." She customarily visits your table after the meal to answer questions about the food and to make sure you leave satisfied. If you plan to eat Thai food, be sure to make reservations. You can order the $12.00, $15.00, or $18.00 dinner with your choice of entrees and soup. Generous portions are served, so the $15.00 dinner should feed any ravenous person. K.O.K. is located at 101 South Main Street in Yazoo City and is open Monday - Saturday, 9:30 am - 9 pm. (601) 746-7997.

THE OLE COUNTRY BAKERY
(Mennonite Bakery)   *Brooksville*

When local folks loyally patronize a business, it should be a tip to travelers that there's something worth stopping for. The Ole Country Bakery in Brooksville is such a place. The sweet earthy aroma of cookies, cakes, and breads drifts through the bakery, tempting the tastebuds of the procession of customers who pass through the front door. The bakery is owned by Geneva Nightengale, of the Mennonite faith, and is staffed by three generations of women who are among the 100 Mennonite families living in the area. Mrs. Nightengale also offers sandwiches prepared with her homemade breads, as well as salads. Located on U.S. Highway 45 and open Tuesday - Saturday from 6 am - 5:30 pm. (601) 738-5795.

LUSCO'S
Greenwood

American restaurant aficionados, Jane and Michael Stern, have proclaimed Lusco's to be "one of the weirdest, and most wonderful, restaurants in America." Charles and Marie Lusco opened a grocery store and a small menu restaurant in 1933, featuring Mama Lusco's spaghetti. Lusco's grew in popularity when Papa Lusco constructed privately partitioned booths where the local gentry could drink his home brew. While the last of the home brew was consumed years ago, the other tradition remains intact. Each party dines behind drawn curtains, and a buzzer is provided to summon the waiter. The restaurant features delicious entrees of seafood, steaks, chicken, and pasta. Lusco's serves imported beer and wine coolers and allows diners to bring their own wine. Steeped in tradition and history, Lusco's merits a trip to Greenwood for an uncommon dining experience. The restaurant is located at 722 Carrolton Avenue and open Tuesday - Saturday from 5:30 pm to 10 pm. Reservations are recommended, but not required. (601) 453-5365.

DOE'S EAT PLACE
Greenville

Doe's Eat Place has received national recognition for serving the best steaks in America. Included among its loyal patrons is President Clinton, who says Doe's is one of his favorite places to dine. Despite all the attention, they've maintained their humbleness. Doe's hasn't changed since it opened in 1941 and doesn't plan to. The restaurant is defiantly unfashionable—operated from a run-down building where diners are seated at a hodgepodge of tables and chairs in one of two small dining rooms or the kitchen. The steaks are the size of hubcaps, cooked to perfection, and served with french-fried potatoes cooked in a cast-iron skillet. The spicy-hot tamales are popular as well. So what's the secret? Since Doe's opened they've operated by a simple philosophy, "Stick to the basics and perfect it"—and they have. The original Doe's is open for dinner Monday - Saturday from 5 pm to 10 pm or so, and located at 502 Nelson, (601) 334-3315. Their second restaurant, Doe's Too, which opened in 1992, serves lunch from 11 am - 2 pm, and dinner from 5 pm to around 9:30 pm. Doe's Too is located at 1551 Highway 1 South in Greenville.

CHAMOUN'S REST HAVEN
Clarksdale

The Delta is full of surprises, and Chamoun's is one of the best. The menu of this seemingly typical southern restaurant reveals exotic dishes of kibbie, stuffed grape leaves, tabouli salad, baklava, and other Lebanese and Mediterranean favorites. Be sure to try the kibbie, Chamoun's most popular dish, which is made from a blend of ground wheat, onions, and seasonings. It can be eaten baked, fried, or raw. Save room for a piece of scrumptious homemade pie, heaped with fluffy meringue. The restaurant is owned by Chafik and Louise Chamoun, who immigrated to the United States in 1954 and settled in Clarksdale. The restaurant is located on U.S. Highway 61 and open Monday - Friday 5 am - 9 pm; Saturday 5:30 am - 9 pm; closed Sunday. (601) 624-8601.

THE CROWN RESTAURANT
Indianola

Five miles north of Indianola, just off State Highway 448, you'll find the Crown Restaurant and Antique Mall, housed in a metal building sitting in the middle of a soybean field. In this most unlikely location, Evelyn and Tony Roughton have created what is probably one of Mississippi's most elegant dining experiences. While waiting to be seated, you can browse through their antique mall, and sample award-winning smoked catfish paté, Evelyn's own creation. You'll dine by candlelight while seated at beautiful English antiques, all of which are for sale. So don't be alarmed if a chair is sold out from under you. The restaurant offers a choice of two equally delicious entrees. Afterwards your server will entice you to sample the dessert table. The choices are absolutely fabulous. The Crown Restaurant serves lunch only from 11:30 am - 1:30 pm, Tuesday - Saturday. (601) 887-2522.

UNCLE HENRY'S PLACE
Moon Lake

"Bates was one of my bright particular beaux! He
got in a quarrel with the wild Wainwright boy.
They shot it out on the floor of Moon Lake Casino."

- Amanda Wingfield in Tennessee Williams' *The Glass Menagarie.*

As a boy, Mississippi native Tennessee Williams visited "Moon
Lake Club" with his grandfather and later immortalized it in several
of his plays. During the 1930s and 1940s, the club was one of the
liveliest nightspots in the Delta, where the area's elite dined, danced,
and risked their fortunes at gambling tables in second-floor rooms.
After the gambling era ended, Henry Trevino opened Uncle Henry's
Place, and now the establishment is operated by his daughter and
grandson, Sarah and George Wright. Today, as Uncle Henry's Place,
cozy beds fill those old casino rooms, and guests can spend the night
in them after a delectable dinner of steak, seafood, and creole dishes.
The lushly planted grounds of Uncle Henry's overlook Moon Lake, a
peaceful, crescent-shaped cut-off of the Mississippi River.

Reservations are required for dinner, which is served Tuesday -
Sunday from 5:30 pm until. Entrees begin at $10.00. Beer is the
only alcoholic beverage served, but guests can bring other spirits.
To get to Uncle Henry's, travel to the junction of U.S. Highways 61
and 49, go west toward Helena for 2.3 miles, turn left onto Moon
Lake Road and go one mile to Uncle Henry's. (601) 337-2757.

THE HOLLYWOOD
Robinsonville

Take U.S. Highway 61 to Robinsonville and follow the signs that
lead to The Hollywood. Stepping through the door of the restaurant
will take you from a tame and tranquil Delta evening to a room
packed with uninhibited people sharing boisterous conversation and
laughter. Patrons maintain a constant stream from their tables to the
dance floor, while quick-footed, cheerful waitresses serve up catfish,
frog legs, steak, and The Hollywood's "original" fried dill pickles.
Housed in an old plantation commissary, the restaurant usually
features live music and serves beer and wine coolers. Guests are
allowed to bring their own spirits, however. Open Thursday, Friday,
and Saturday from 6 pm to 11:30 pm. Reservations are required, but

a table might be found if you happen to be passing through that corner of the Delta. Phone (601) 363-1126.

THE BLUE & WHITE
Tunica

A day at Tunica's Blue & White restaurant dawns at 5 am when waitresses begin serving sleepy-eyed farmers hearty breakfasts and gallons of hot coffee. Their breakfast of grits, eggs, red-eye gravy and a piece of ham too large to fit on the plate, should hold any diner through the morning until the Blue & White serves up its blue-plate-special lunch. Evening dinner and Sunday lunches are popular as well for restaurant owners Wiley and Earline Chambers. Opened in 1937, the restaurant and service station has grown into a local landmark, serving up hot coffee, savory southern vittles, and constant conversation from 5 am to 10 pm. Located on U.S. Highway 61. (601) 363-1371.

SMITTY'S
Oxford

Smitty's is everything a small-town southern cafe should be, and more. Each morning a potpourri of people, from townsfolk to university students, gather over breakfasts of coffee, grits, and biscuits to discuss everything from last night's high school football game to the work of William Faulkner, the town's celebrated writer. Although breakfast is the high point at Smitty's, their southern-style lunch and dinner menu is also popular. The waitresses at Smitty's are good ambassadors of southern hospitality; even if you're just passing through, they'll make you feel like a regular. After eating, stop next door at Square Books to browse in one of the state's best bookstores. Smitty's is located at 208 S. Lamar, just off the Courthouse Square, and open Monday - Saturday from 6 am to 9 pm, Sunday from 8 am - 9 pm. (601) 234-9111.

TAYLOR GROCERY & RESTAURANT
Taylor

While traveling in Mississippi, you'll notice we have an abundance of "catfish houses." Most of the restaurants are similar in design,and it's rare to be served a below-par plate of Mississippi's favorite fish.

But for a unique catfish dinner, drive 10 miles south of Oxford, and in the curve of a narrow country road, you'll find Taylor, population 301. This backroads hamlet is known for being home to some of Mississippi's finest artists—and for the catfish. The Taylor Grocery & Restaurant serves up steamy-hot and flavorful catfish trimmed with hush-puppies, french fries, and cole slaw. The unmatching vinyl tablecloths and chairs, bare-bulb lighting, and graffiti-covered walls create an amiable and unassuming atmosphere. Dining hours are Thursday - Sunday from 5:30 pm to 10 pm. BYOB. (601) 236-1716.

COMO STEAK HOUSE
Como

Halfway between Senatobia and Sardis, off Interstate 55, you'll find the small town of Como, home of the Como Steakhouse. Housed in what was once an old general store and post office, the restaurant is a favorite of beef-eaters in northwest Mississippi. For the price of $15.95, you'll be served one of their tender, juicy steaks. Your choices include, but aren't limited to, a 24-ounce T- bone, 24-ounce sirloin, and a 17-ounce ribeye. All dinners are served with a salad, baked potato, and garlic toast. For $11.00 each you can split a steak with a friend. The steaks are cooked on an open grill in one of the three dining rooms, and patrons can even cook their own and take a dollar off the price of the their meal. Chicken and catfish dinners are also available. Located at 203 Main Street and open Tuesday - Saturday from 5 pm to 10:30 pm. Wine and mixed drinks are available. (601) 526-9529.

PHILLIPS GROCERY
Holly Springs

A secret recipe that's been kept under wraps since 1948 won Phillips Grocery national fame in 1989, when *USA Today* hailed their burger as one of the top three "Perfect Burgers" in the nation. Phillips is worth a visit for more than just good burgers. The two-story building was constructed in 1882 across from a beautiful railroad depot, and operated as a saloon until Prohibition in 1919. Today, it serves nothing stronger than soda pop. Located at 541-A Van Dorn Avenue in Holly Springs. Open Monday 9 am - 3 pm; Tuesday - Saturday 9 am - 6 pm. (601) 252-4671.

BILL'S HAMBURGERS
Amory

It's not tough to decide what to eat when you go to Bill's because you only get burgers, and they only come one of two ways, "with or without"—onions, that is. Since 1929 the citizens of Amory have devoured thousands of these burgers, which simply offer real beef, a bun, and onions or not. Ketchup, mustard, and hot sauce are available, but nothing else. In keeping with the no-frills approach, burger lovers are seated at bar stools that surround the cooking area and eat off the wax paper that covers their burgers.

Although the restaurant has changed hands several times, the burgers have remained exactly the same for 64 years. A single burger is $1.10, a double is $1.65 and French fries are 75 cents. The restaurant is located on Main Street at Vinegar Bend in Amory, and open 7 am - 5:30 pm, Monday - Friday and 7 am - 5 pm on Saturday. (601) 256-2085.

DRUG STORE SODA FOUNTAINS

Escape from the modern fast-food jungles to an oasis of friendly people enjoying the simple things in life. Cherry sprites, banana splits, and slow-sizzling burgers await you at these havens of nostalgia and charm. The gleaming stainless steel, neighborly chatter of townspeople, and tall twirling stools will transport you to a bygone era.

Borroum's Drug Store, Corinth - Founded in 1865 by Dr. A.J. Borroum, a surgeon in the Confederate Army; open 6 am to 7 pm, Monday - Sunday; located at 604 Walron Street.

Brent's Drugs, Jackson - Opened in 1947; located next to the Jitney Jungle on Duling Avenue in north Jackson's Woodland Hills Shopping Center; the soda fountain is open from 7:30 am to 4:30 pm.

Parkins Drug Store, Jackson - Located in the Belhaven area next to the Jitney Jungle on Fortification Street; has been at its present location since 1965; open 8 am - 5 pm, Monday - Saturday.

Calvert-Carraway Pharmacy, Biloxi - Located at 2400 Pass Road; founded in 1962; the fountain is open from 8 am to 3 pm, Monday - Saturday, and 8:30 am to noon on Sundays.

Triplett-Day Drug Store, Gulfport - Opened in 1955; located at 25th Avenue (Hwy 49) and 14th Street; serves blue-plate-special lunches as well as breakfast and sodas; serves food from 8 am to 2 pm and sodas until 6 pm, Monday - Friday. The store closes at 4 pm on Saturdays.

Bug Jam

Index

Lorraine Redd traveled over 13,000 miles of Mississippi back-roads to compile the material for her travel guide. Ms. Redd is a native of Laurel and a graduate of the University of Southern Mississippi. *Only in Mississippi* is her first book.